The Berenstain Bears

The Whole Year Through

The Berenstain Bears

The Whole Year Through

Stan & Jan Berenstain

WITH EARTHSAVER TIPS
AND THINGS TO DO FOR EACH AND
EVERY MONTH OF THE YEAR

Cartwheel
B·O·O·K·S ®

SCHOLASTIC INC.
New York Toronto London Auckland Sydney

Library of Congress Cataloging-in-Publication Data

Berenstain, Stan.
    The Berenstain Bears the whole year through : with earthsaver tips and things to do for each and every month of the year / by Stan and Jan Berenstain.
        p.   cm.
    Summary: Presents poems, environmentally friendly advice, and information about nature for each month of the year.
    ISBN 0-590-95693-0
    1. Environmental protection—Citizen participation—Juvenile literature.   2. Natural history—Juvenile literature.   [1. Months. 2. Nature study. 3. Environmental protection.] I. Berenstain, Jan.   II. Title.
TD171.7.B46   1998
508—dc21   96-38778
                                                                                                         CIP
                                                                                                         AC

12 11 10 9 8 7 6 5 4 3 2   8 9/9 0/0 01 02

Printed in the U.S.A.   08

First Scholastic printing, January 1998

IT'S JANUARY!
The time has come
for resolution.
Let's all resolve
to stop pollution.

· RESOLUTION ·

Mama, Papa, Sister, Brother,
we appreciate each other,
and we all appreciate
the things that make our planet great.

We show our deep appreciation
for Mother Nature's grand creation
by doing the things we ought to do.
We are sure that you do, too!

A recycled milk carton reduces trash and helps birds weather winter storms.

WHERE'S MY HAT?

TEMPORARILY RECYCLED!

OW TO MAKE AN NVIRONMENTALLY AFE SNOW BEAR:

SAFE:
walnuts, acorns, pinecones

UNSAFE:
plastic balls, buttons

Nuts and seeds feed our forest friends and start new growth. Plastic pollutes the Earth forever.

WARNING:
Icicles are not ice pops. One lick of some frozen roof runoff convinces Sister Bear. UGH!

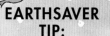

bird seed

stale bread

suet (fat)

GREAT HEAD, MAMA! NOW ROLL UP A BODY!

· BIRDS IN WINTER ·

In February, when chill winds freeze
your toes and nose and ears and knees,
remember these important words:
Do not forget to feed the birds.

Give them bread crumbs, seed, and suet.
Don't put it off, get out and DO IT!

TRY THIS:
Chill a sheet of black paper in the freezer to catch snowflakes on. You may glimpse their beautiful crystalline shapes.

THINGS TO DO WITH SNOW:

Make angel shapes.

Build a fort.

Sled on it.

SOMETHING *NOT* TO DO WITH SNOW: Catch it on your tongue. Snow falling through polluted air picks up things that aren't good for you.

IT'S MARCH!
From mighty trees
to lowly weeds,
March winds spread
life's precious seeds.

•NATURE'S SCHEME•

When in March you long for May,
and March winds blow your hat away,
remember this important theme:
It's all part of Nature's scheme.
Those seeds that March winds
    spread o'er Earth
help give the spring and summer birth.

WELCOME MARCH BY MAKING A KITE

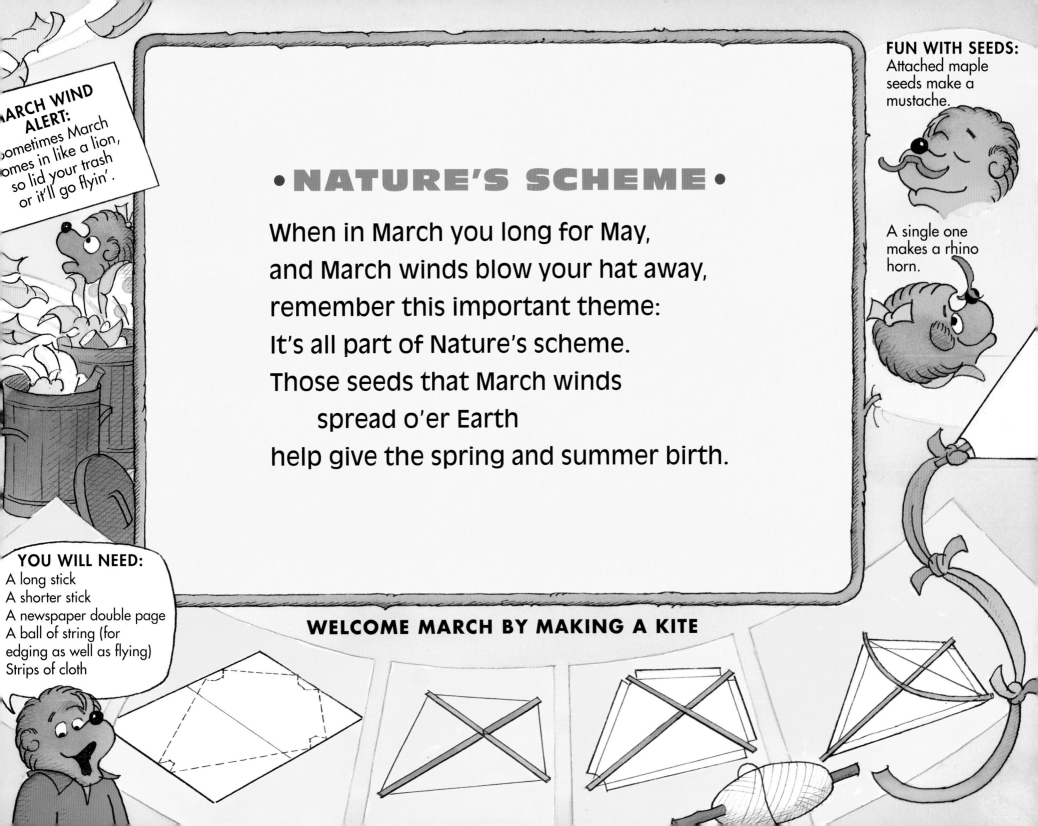

·RAIN, RAIN, DON'T GO AWAY·

"Rain, rain, go away," is as wrong as it can be.

For to water the Earth is rain's decree.

It waters every seedling, every plant and tree,

every bulb and flower; it waters you and me.

It may splish-splash the Earth to muck,

but without rain, we'd be out of luck.

Which is why we say:

"Rain, rain, go away," is as wrong as it can be!

ISN'T IT FUNNY HOW BEES MAKE HONEY?

FUNNY, NOTHING, YOU SILLY BEAR. IT TAKES A LOT OF WORK AND CARE!

It takes the work of many thousands of bees to make a single jar of honey.

IT'S MAY!
Plants and creatures
all give birth.
For all our sakes,
let's save the Earth!

•MORE THAN FLOWERS!•

In the month of May, Mother Earth

does her job for all she's worth.

No ifs, ands, buts, or maybes,

the month of May means babies.

Cats have kittens, dogs have puppies,

guppy moms have baby guppies.

Frogs and toads and their tads

swim among the lily pads.

Deer have fawns, hens have chicks,

mice have mice, ticks have ticks.

No ifs, ands, buts, or maybes,

The month of May means . . .

BABIES!

Pick a seed puff.
Blow on it. Count
the seeds that
remain and add
o'clock. It may
not be accurate,
but it's fun.

ZINNIA

PETUNIA

MARIGOLD

COSMOS

DAISY

PANSY

Annuals (flowers that
you plant every year)
make lots of seeds. Your
seed-eating friends
will visit your garden
all summer for them.

IT'S JUNE!
Earth prepares
all the year
to give us summer —
NOW IT'S HERE!

ARTHSAVER
TIP:

plastic drink
ers as shown
re you throw
hem away . . .

o they can't
onto the
s of birds and
ws of fish
prevent them
eating.

· SCHOOL'S OUT ·

No more pencils, no more books,

no more teachers' dirty looks.

No more bus rides, no more gym,

no more feeling dumb or dim.

No more Show, no more Tell,

no more waiting for the bell.

For while school is not a total bummer,

it can't begin to compare with . . .

SUMMER!

EEK!

All of us are
Great Earth's guests,
even those
considered pests.

IT'S A
RAID!

Many creatures we think of
as pests help us every
day. For example, there
are about 40,000 kinds
of spiders. They eat
the more pesky pests
that carry disease and
that destroy trees, plants,
and food.

•A SUMMER'S NIGHT•

Behold the night, its moonlit drama,
a deep and darkling diorama,
all strewn with stars light-years away,
distant suns unseen by day.
The soundless, boundless flight of bats,
the seeking song of lovelorn cats,
the mosquitoes' itchy vampire whine,
finding hosts on whom to dine.
Behold the night, its moonlit drama,
a deep and darkling diorama.

THINGS TO COLLECT IN SUMMER:

leaves   stones   feathers   shells

SOMETHING *NOT* TO COLLECT:
nests! Many kinds of birds like "recycled" nests, so leave them for the birds.

THE MIRACLE
F THE
ONARCH:

he amazing
onarch butterfly
es thousands
f miles between
lew England and
entral America
very year.

WHAT'S A
MIRACLE,
PAPA?

A MIRACLE
IS SOMETHING
WONDERFUL WE
CANNOT QUITE
EXPLAIN.

•OUR FRIEND, THE SUN•

When it rises from horizon's bed,

it's just a sliver, tomato red.

Next, an orange, cut in two,

arcing now across the blue,

o'er the sunflower's yellow face,

the creamy white of Queen Anne's lace,

the orange of a monarch's wings,

the colors of so many things.

Now, it's setting in the west,

sinking 'neath horizon's crest.

Once again, a sliver red,

our friend, the sun, has gone to bed.

EARTHSAVER
TIP:
Use the Bag
Return stations
at your
supermarket and
help save whole
forests.

BAG
RETURN

THANK YOU,
EARTHSAVERS!

WOW!
MOTHER NATURE
CERTAINLY HAS
A GREEN
THUMB!

Don't throw
away last year's
notebooks. The
unused pages are
good for practice
and sketching.

And don't throw
away those pencil
nubs. If we all use
pencil extenders,
thousands of trees
will be saved.

• SEPTEMBER IS WHEN . . . •

Birds begin their southward flight.

Days grow shorter than the night.

We put away our bat and mitt.

We make sure our soccer jerseys fit.

We note the autumnal equinox.

We say goodbye to hollyhocks.

We say hello to chrysanthemums.

We cut the last rose and prick our thumbs.

Evenings are turning a little cool.

We think about going back to school.

We sigh for summer, mostly gone.

We and the seasons are moving on.

Prepare for
later gift-giving
by drying some
flowers and
grasses. Tie up
small bunches
and hang them
upside down in
a dry place.

Make wreaths out
of wild-grape vines
and leave them in
the sun to dry.
You'll be ready
for gift-giving
time in December.

HOW TO WATCH FOR BATS:

Stare at the sky just before dark.
If you're lucky, you'll see the zigzag
flight of bats catching their evening
meal. They're among the most
helpful animal friends we have.
They eat millions of mosquitoes
and gnats every single night of
the long summer.

RECYCLING PAPER BAGS AT HALLOWEEN:

...ake masks! They ...n be as scary ... you want to ...ake them. Be ...re to cut out ...g eyeholes ...d a few extra ...rholes.

• BOO! •

There's more to October than bright blue weather.

There are Halloween parties, getting together,

dressing up and trick-or-treating,

eating your goodies at a single seating.

It's haunted houses, ghostly moans,

and skeletons dancing around in their bones.

It's witches streaking across the skies.

It's hideous, horrible bloodcurdling cries.

And then, when it's over, climbing into your bed

and pulling the covers up over your head.

MUM'S THE WORD!

Autumn is even more colorful with chrysanthemums. And they're perennial! (Once you plant them, they come up year after year.)

THINGS TO DO WITH BALLOONS:

Make a punching bag.

Paint funny faces on them.

Play indoor volleyball. (Ask a grown-up to set up a toilet-paper or paper-towel net.)

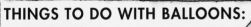

SOMETHING *NOT* TO DO WITH BALLOONS:
Let helium-filled ones fly away.

Fish and other animals swallow them when they deflate over water.

EARTHSAVER SHOPPING TIP:

Ask your parents to buy eggs in cardboard boxes when available.

cardboard

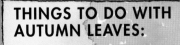

plastic

CARDBOARD IS BIODEGRADABLE. PLASTIC IS NOT.

· THANKFULNESS ·

It was time for the Bears' Thanksgiving dinner.

They sat down to a meal that was truly a winner.

There was gravy and stuffing and marshmallow yams,

corn-on-the-cob and jellies and jams,

a golden-brown turkey with savory spices,

two kinds of pie and fresh fruit ices.

After the meal, Pa offered a toast,

"We're thankful for dinner. It was really the most!"

"You're welcome," said Mama. "But I must confess,

I will be thankful if you clean up the mess!"

HOW TO WISH UPON A BONE:

To use the wishbone of your Thanksgiving turkey, first pick it clean, let it dry for three days, then ask another cub to wish with you, and *yank.* If you break off the big half, you get your wish!

THINGS TO DO WITH AUTUMN LEAVES:

Admire them.

Use them to make mulch (fallen leaves combined with other organic material) for the garden.

Jump in them!

SOMETHING *NOT* TO DO WITH AUTUMN LEAVES:

Burn them.

Not only does leaf burning pollute the air, but in many places it's against the law!

IT'S DECEMBER!
The Christmas star
so high and bright
fills our lives
with a thousand
points of light!

EARTHSAVER GIFT IDEA (CONTINUED):

s time to follow
with your dried
owers and
reaths project.
ke clusters of the
owers into the
reaths. Add
necones and
ribbons!

• THE CHRISTMAS STAR •

The Christmas star, it says to us,
there's more to Christmas than the fuss.
There's kindness, love, and warmth, God bless,
squeezes, hugs, and happiness.
The Christmas star reminds us all
to love Earth's creatures great and small—
not just bears like me and you,
but all its other creatures, too—
and the Earth itself, with all our might,
through every blessed day and night.

EARTHSAVER GIFT-WRAP IDEA:

Bright and colorful, recycled and *free*—the Sunday funnies!

CELEBRATE THE HOLIDAYS WITH SANTA APPLE TAFFIES:

Ask a grown-up to make candied apples. While holding them by their sticks, decorate them with mini-marshmallows and gumdrops to look like Santa!